John Locke: How Philosophy Shapes The Human Mind.

Philosophical compendiums, Volume 4

Rodrigo v. santos

Published by Pomar Assets, 2025.

While every precaution has been taken in the preparation of this book, the publisher assumes no responsibility for errors or omissions, or for damages resulting from the use of the information contained herein.

JOHN LOCKE: HOW PHILOSOPHY SHAPES THE HUMAN MIND.

First edition. March 3, 2025.

Copyright © 2025 Rodrigo v. santos.

ISBN: 979-8230014195

Written by Rodrigo v. santos.

Table of Contents

Who Was John Locke?.. 1
Introduction: 2
"An Essay Concerning Human Understanding" (1690) 3
"Two Treatises of Government" (1689) 9
"Thoughts on Education" (1693) 14
A Letter Concerning Toleration - 1689..................................20
"Some Thoughts Concerning the Consequences of the Lowering of Interest and the Raising of the Value of Money" (1691)..26
"A Project for a New Coin" (Some Considerations of the Consequences of the Lowering of Interest and the Raising of the Value of Money) - 1691 32
    Constitution of Carolina – 1669 37
    A Second Letter Concerning Toleration (1690) 43
    "Civil Government" (1680)..48
    "Reasonableness of Christianity" (1695) 53
    "Human Reason" - 1690 57
    "Economic Writings" 62
    Final Notes:..67
    Bibliographic references:..68

"I would like to first dedicate this work to my beloved savior who watches over all of us, and to the teams who created all the digital tools necessary for the production of this and many other beautiful works, my thanks."

Who Was John Locke?

John Locke (1632–1704) was an English philosopher whose ideas played a fundamental role in the development of modern political and philosophical thought. Born in Wrington, Somerset, Locke was educated at Oxford and dedicated much of his life to study and writing. He is best known for his work *An Essay Concerning Human Understanding*, in which he advocates the empiricist theory of the mind, arguing that the mind is a "blank slate" at birth and that experience is the primary source of knowledge.

Additionally, Locke had a significant influence on political ideas, especially in his work *Two Treatises of Government*. In these writings, he defended the concept of the social contract and the separation of powers, ideas that later became central to the formation of democratic governments. Locke believed that individuals have natural rights, including life, liberty, and property, and that the government should exist to protect these rights.

Locke also actively participated in the debates of his time, contributing to religious tolerance and the idea that political power should be limited to protect individual rights. His influence extended far beyond his era, shaping the foundations of Enlightenment thought and inspiring the drafting of the United States Declaration of Independence. In summary, John Locke was a seminal figure in the history of political philosophy and a champion of individual liberty and democratic principles.

Introduction:

John Locke was one of the most influential philosophers of the 17th century, whose ideas profoundly shaped political, economic, and social thought. His work offers deep reflections on themes such as human nature, freedom, government, and property rights. Throughout this book, we aim to make some of his most complex ideas accessible and clear, without losing sight of their continued relevance in modern society. Our goal is to simplify and organize his concepts so that any reader, regardless of prior knowledge, can understand his fundamental ideas.

Locke believed in the importance of human reason and individual freedom, arguing that all individuals possess inalienable natural rights to life, liberty, and property. He also addressed the role of government, proposing that political authority could only be legitimized through the consent of the governed. With these ideas, Locke offered a new perspective on the relationship between the citizen and the state, influencing not only the political thought of his time but also the revolutions that followed, such as the American Revolution.

Drawing from Locke's major works, such as *Two Treatises of Government* and *An Essay Concerning Human Understanding*, we explore his contributions in a direct and simplified manner, highlighting his most significant concepts. This book does not seek to be a deep academic analysis but rather an accessible and engaging introduction to Locke's ideas, allowing readers to gain a clear understanding of the lasting impact of his thought on the modern world.

"An Essay Concerning Human Understanding" (1690)

John Locke's *An Essay Concerning Human Understanding*, a masterpiece of intellectual inquiry, stands as a philosophical beacon of the 17th century. First published in 1690, Locke's treatise offers a profound and comprehensive exploration of the human mind, establishing itself as a seminal work in British empiricism. In this philosophical endeavor, Locke challenges the prevailing doctrine of innate ideas, meticulously constructing his epistemological theory with precision and insight.

The *Essay* is structured into four books, each contributing to an overarching vision of human understanding. In Book I, Locke refutes the doctrine of innate ideas, arguing that the mind is a *tabula rasa* at birth, receptive only to sensory impressions from the external world. This opposition to the prevailing orthodoxy lays the foundation for an empiricist approach that illuminates the process of idea formation.

Book II delves into the origins and classification of ideas, undertaking a meticulous investigation that extends beyond a mere exposition of concepts. Locke categorizes ideas as simple or complex, distinguishing between those derived from sensory experience and those formed through mental operations. His detailed taxonomy provides a solid framework for understanding the complexity of human thought.

Book III focuses on language, offering a profound treatise on communication and the expression of knowledge. Locke examines the nuances of language, linking words directly to the ideas formed in the mind. His analysis of words as vehicles of meaning and his emphasis on clarity in communication anticipate concepts that would later influence linguistic theories and philosophical discourse.

Finally, Book IV ventures into the realm of epistemology, where Locke explores the nature and limits of human knowledge. His reflections on certainty and the scope of human understanding provide a nuanced perspective on cognitive capacities, contributing to an epistemological framework that remains relevant to this day.

Beyond his philosophical insight, Locke meticulously examines the relationship between ideas and the qualities of objects. In Book II, he articulates a crucial distinction between primary and secondary qualities. The former—such as extension, shape, and motion—reside objectively in objects, independent of human perception. The latter—such as color and taste—are inherently subjective, existing only within individual sensory experience. This carefully outlined dichotomy serves as a cornerstone for understanding the nature of ideas and the role of experience in their formation.

A central element of Locke's epistemology is his theory of representation. He conceives the mind as a reflective mirror, capturing sensory impressions and reproducing them as ideas. This concept is crucial to understanding how knowledge originates and develops. Locke's masterful exposition of this process culminates in a sophisticated view of the mind as an active and dynamic repository of experience.

Another remarkable aspect of *An Essay Concerning Human Understanding* is Locke's emphasis on religious and political tolerance, a theme that echoes in his later political writings. With a visionary perspective, he advocates for the separation of civil and religious domains, defending freedom of conscience as a fundamental right. His argument, grounded in the limitations of governmental power and the necessity of preserving individual rights, foreshadows Enlightenment principles that would shape modern democratic foundations.

Locke's epistemological contributions extend beyond the analysis of idea formation to a deeper exploration of belief and certainty. In Book IV, he navigates the complex terrain of knowledge theory, examining varying degrees of certainty and the extent of human comprehension. With keen insight, Locke argues that absolute certainty is reserved for a few self-evident truths, while most propositions exist within a spectrum of probability and conviction. This nuanced approach reveals the depth of his thought, offering an analysis that transcends simplistic dichotomies.

One of Locke's most enduring contributions lies in his theory of representation, which is fundamental to understanding not only the formation of ideas but also how these ideas evolve into knowledge. For Locke, the mind acts as a mirror reflecting external reality, but this reflection is not passive. The mind actively interprets sensory impressions, organizing and transforming them into coherent ideas. This dynamic and interactive conception of the mind anticipates key insights in cognitive psychology and continues to influence contemporary theories on knowledge construction.

Another salient point in Locke's work is his differentiation between the various degrees of knowledge. He distinguishes between intuitive, demonstrative, and sensitive knowledge. Intuitive knowledge, characterized by immediate certainty, applies to self-evident truths. Demonstrative knowledge, attained through logical inferences, encompasses more complex propositions. Sensitive knowledge, derived from sensory experience, constitutes the majority of our understanding of the world. This tripartite classification provides a detailed analysis of the different layers of human cognition, adding crucial nuances to Lockean epistemology.

The political and social significance of Locke's ideas in *An Essay Concerning Human Understanding* cannot be overstated. His strong advocacy for tolerance, the separation of religious and civil spheres, and his emphasis on individual liberty transcend the boundaries of philosophy, shaping the trajectory of modern political thought. With a vision ahead of his time, Locke sows the seeds for the emergence of liberal democracy and individual rights, thus contributing to the ideological foundation of contemporary societies.

As Locke explores the final books of *An Essay Concerning Human Understanding*, he not only outlines a comprehensive theory of the human mind but also provides an in-depth analysis of the origins of language and its implications for communication and knowledge development. In Book III, the philosopher delves into the complexities of language, emphasizing its intrinsic connection to ideas and the necessity of clarity in expression. By examining the relationship between words and ideas, Locke anticipates linguistic considerations that would later resonate in semantic and pragmatic theories.

Locke's attention to language extends beyond its superficial structure to a deeper understanding of words as instruments for conveying meaning. For Locke, clarity in communication is not merely a stylistic concern but a fundamental requirement for the effective exchange of thoughts and, consequently, for the advancement of knowledge. His emphasis on language as a mediator of thought underscores his holistic approach, which connects epistemology to pragmatics, highlighting the intrinsic relationship between theory and practice.

In the political sphere, Locke's ideas in his later writings echo the principles introduced in *An Essay Concerning Human Understanding*. His defense of the separation between civil and religious power, manifested in *A Letter Concerning Toleration*, envisions a pluralistic society that respects individual differences. This political engagement reflects not only a practical application of his philosophical principles but also a significant contribution to the development of democratic governance and constitutional principles that remain fundamental to contemporary democracies.

The lasting impact of *An Essay Concerning Human Understanding* is undeniable. Locke's ideas on knowledge formation, the nature of the mind, and language continue to challenge and inspire scholars across diverse fields, including philosophy, cognitive psychology, and political theory. His influence transcends disciplinary boundaries, shaping the intellectual fabric of societies that uphold freedom, tolerance, and the relentless pursuit of human understanding.

In summary, John Locke's *An Essay Concerning Human Understanding* emerges not only as a masterful philosophical treatise but as a monumental work that transcends time and discipline. His meticulous examination of the human mind, his theory of representation, his analysis of language, and his political vision collectively contribute to a legacy that enriches our understanding of thought and the foundations of contemporary societies. Locke remains a towering figure in the intellectual history of humanity, whose ideas continue to resonate and inspire successive generations of thinkers.

"Two Treatises of Government" (1689)

"*Two Treatises of Government"*, the seminal work of the English philosopher John Locke, is a cornerstone in the development of modern political thought. Originally published in 1689, the work serves as a powerful response to the absolute monarchy of the time, offering a compelling defense of natural rights and the theory of the social contract.

Locke, influenced by empiricism and the political context of his era, constructs a sophisticated argument that still resonates in contemporary debates on governance and individual rights. The first treatise addresses the origin and legitimacy of political power, rejecting the notion of the divine right of kings and asserting that political power derives from the consent of the governed. By advocating for a social contract, Locke argues that individuals, in their natural state, possess inalienable natural rights, including life, liberty, and property. These rights serve as the foundation for the justification of political authority, which, according to Locke, must exist to preserve these individual prerogatives.

In the second treatise, Locke delves deeper into the nature of political power and the limitations that should be placed on government. He proposes the separation of legislative and executive powers to prevent abuses of authority. This division of powers, which later influenced the drafting of the United States Constitution, clearly reflects Locke's belief in the importance of establishing safeguards against tyranny.

Locke's language is characteristically clear and accessible, reflecting his commitment to communicating his ideas not only to academics but also to the general public. His argumentation, while grounded in philosophical principles, is rooted in practical examples and observations of human nature. This pragmatic approach contributes to the enduring relevance of his work, which has transcended temporal and cultural boundaries.

However, it is crucial to recognize the criticisms directed at Locke's arguments. Some scholars question his optimistic view of human nature, suggesting that his perspective may be overly idealized. Furthermore, the practical application of his theories in the modern world has been the subject of debate, particularly regarding the interpretation and implementation of property rights.

Locke's lasting influence is not without controversy. Contemporary critics raise concerns about the universality of his principles, emphasizing the specific 17th-century context in which he developed his theories. The direct applicability of Locke's ideas in complex and diverse societies is frequently debated, especially when confronted with the challenges of the contemporary world.

One of the central points of discussion is Locke's emphasis on property as a fundamental right. While some see this perspective as essential for preserving individual freedom and encouraging economic development, others argue that an excessive focus on property can lead to socioeconomic inequalities and the marginalization of certain groups in society. The inherent complexity of interpreting and applying these principles reflects the constantly evolving nature of social dynamics.

Additionally, Locke's treatise has been critically examined for its stance on slavery. Despite his vigorous defense of natural rights, Locke remains notably ambiguous regarding slavery, raising questions about the consistency of his application of the principles of freedom and equality. This ambiguity highlights contradictions within Locke's political thought and prompts reflections on the limitations of his concepts when faced with complex ethical issues.

The contemporary resonance of Locke's ideas is also evident in debates on government legitimacy and the extent of individual rights in the face of perceived national security threats. The tension between preserving individual freedom and the necessity of a strong state to maintain public order continues to challenge policymakers and political theorists today.

Thus, Locke's work serves as a fruitful starting point for exploring and understanding political dilemmas that persist in contemporary society. Another critical point of reflection regarding Locke's work lies in his conception of the state of nature. The philosopher's optimistic view of human nature, marked by an assumed predisposition toward reason and the pursuit of life and property preservation, is often contested.

Critics argue that this idealized vision may overlook the complexities of human behavior, including the capacity for violence and disorder. The tension between the idealization of the state of nature as a state of freedom and equality and the need for government to mitigate human conflicts remains an enduring interpretive challenge. Furthermore, Locke's emphasis on property as a fundamental right sparks debates on the social and economic implications of his theory.

While some interpret property protection as a crucial safeguard for individual freedom and economic development, others argue that this emphasis can contribute to the perpetuation of socioeconomic inequalities. The dynamic between freedom and equality, central to contemporary political reflections, provides fertile ground for a critical reassessment of Locke's contributions.

The timelessness of Locke's themes is evident in the ongoing debates over government legitimacy and the scope of individual rights. The ethical and political dilemmas faced by modern governments, such as protecting national security while addressing concerns about civil rights, echo the discussions initiated by Locke. His advocacy for limiting governmental power and separating powers continues to resonate in contemporary political structures, yet the nuances of these applications remain a challenge for effective interpretation and implementation.

The interpretation of Locke's work also raises questions about his view of the legislative power as a mechanism for protecting natural rights. While Locke strongly defends representation and popular participation in legislation as means of safeguarding individual rights, contemporary critics point to the inherent challenges of democratic practice, including the potential for tyranny of the majority and the marginalization of minorities. These reflections resonate in debates about the effectiveness of democratic systems in protecting fundamental rights in increasingly complex societies.

Additionally, analyzing the implications of Locke's theories for international relations and global governance is an area of considerable critical interest. Locke's emphasis on sovereignty and the social contract within national borders raises questions about the applicability of his principles in an interconnected global context. The intersection between national autonomy and international cooperation, particularly in issues such as human rights and climate change, challenges the direct application of Locke's ideas and highlights the need for adaptation to address contemporary global-scale challenges.

The dialogue between Locke's ideas and subsequent political philosophies, such as those of Rousseau and Kant, also provides a rich field for critical analysis. The tensions between individualistic and communal conceptions of rights and duties, as well as the divergences on the nature of freedom, have echoed throughout philosophical and political discussions in history. Locke's work, therefore, not only represents a starting point but also a point of intersection in the evolution of Western political thought.

Ultimately, *Two Treatises of Government* by John Locke challenges readers to move beyond uncritical admiration. The richness of his contribution to political theory is undeniable, but critical analysis is essential to explore the nuances, ambiguities, and limitations inherent in his approach. Like every foundational thinker, Locke invites constant reflection and the sensitive application of his ideas in a dynamic and multifaceted world, where the intersection between theory and practice continues to shape the course of governance and human coexistence.

"Thoughts on Education" (1693)

"*Thoughts on Education,*" John Locke's seminal work, presents a keen and profound analysis of the foundations of education, outlining principles that transcend the temporal context in which it was written. Locke, one of the most influential thinkers in 17th-century political philosophy, bases his educational reflections on an empiricist approach, reinforcing the idea that the human mind is a *"tabula rasa,"* a blank slate shaped by sensory experiences.

The core of Locke's argument rests on the premise that education is crucial for the moral and intellectual development of the individual. His advocacy for the promotion of knowledge through direct experience and observation as vehicles for acquiring understanding is articulated with an eloquence that resonates through the ages. With mastery, Locke sketches the concept that the mind, at birth, is a blank page, emphasizing the importance of education as the formative and refining force of personality.

Throughout the work, Locke outlines a comprehensive educational plan, addressing everything from childhood care to formal instruction. His emphasis on the individuality of the learner, their abilities, and inclinations permeates his reflections, asserting that education must be tailored to the peculiarities of each student. This forward-thinking approach echoes in contemporary times, inspiring educational theories that recognize the diversity of learning.

Locke's critique of authoritarian educational practices and mechanical memorization highlights his progressive vision. His appeal for intellectual freedom, encouraging independent thought and the development of discernment, stands out as a crucial contribution to understanding the role of education in shaping autonomous citizens. However, it is imperative to acknowledge that Locke's vision, while innovative for his time, may be considered limited in some aspects due to the lack of a stronger emphasis on education for citizenship and the promotion of social values. His focus on the individual may, in certain contexts, overlook the importance of fostering a cohesive and ethical society.

Another notable aspect of Locke's work is his conception of education as a means to promote not only intellectual capacity but also virtue. By grounding moral formation in reason, he underscores the importance of cultivating ethical understanding from youth. This approach, which seeks to balance cognitive development with the construction of a solid ethical foundation, resonates with contemporary discussions on the holistic formation of individuals.

Locke's pragmatic approach to education also deserves attention. He recognizes the importance of practical and utilitarian instruction, geared toward real-world demands. His vision of education as preparation for the practical challenges of daily life aligns remarkably with modern needs in a constantly evolving society. However, it is vital to point out the limitations of his work regarding educational equity. Although Locke advocates for the right to education, he does not extensively address socioeconomic disparities that may hinder equal access to instruction. This gap in his approach highlights the need to complement his ideas with a deeper analysis of social justice issues in education.

Furthermore, Locke's emphasis on education as a means to form law-abiding citizens and obedience to authority can be interpreted as a reflection of his time, marked by political and social changes. However, this emphasis can be questioned in a contemporary world that values critical civic participation and responsible questioning of power structures. Additionally, it is interesting to note how Locke's vision of teaching, although grounded in reason and experience, could be enriched by a deeper consideration of the social and cultural dimensions of learning. His emphasis on direct observation and experimentation, while valuable, may neglect the importance of cultural context in the formation of knowledge.

Multiculturalism and the diversity of experiences present in contemporary society demand an educational approach that goes beyond the universality proposed by Locke, incorporating diverse perspectives and valuing the richness of cultural plurality. Another crucial point to consider is the relevance of Locke's work in the context of digital education today. The technological revolution has radically transformed learning methods, and Locke's experience-centered approach can be reinterpreted in light of technological innovations. As technology plays an increasingly predominant role in education, it would be relevant to explore how Locke's principles adapt to and influence educational practices in a digital environment, considering the opportunities and challenges presented by this new era.

Nevertheless, it is crucial to recognize Locke's enduring influence on the development of educational theories and political thought. His defense of individual freedom, combined with an optimistic view of human potential, continues to resonate in debates about the purpose of education in shaping autonomous citizens. By conceiving education as a means to enhance not only intellect but also morality, Locke establishes a foundation that transcends temporal boundaries, stimulating critical reflections on the transformative role of education in society.

Moreover, it is relevant to consider the resonance of Locke's ideas in the context of contemporary theories on cognitive and educational development. His emphasis on education as a continuous process, shaped by experiences and interactions, finds an echo in modern approaches such as constructivist theory. The idea that learning is an active endeavor in which individuals construct their knowledge through interaction with the environment remains a central pillar in many contemporary educational theories.

However, a pertinent critique of Locke's work lies in the lack of a deeper exploration of emotional dimensions in the educational process. The author's emphasis on reason and observation may seem to overlook the importance of emotions in knowledge formation. Contemporary approaches, such as emotional intelligence, highlight the need to integrate emotional dimensions into education, recognizing that cognitive development is intrinsically linked to emotional balance.

Another aspect worthy of critical analysis is Locke's view on women's education. Although his emphasis on education for virtue applies to both men and women, his approach can be interpreted as perpetuating traditional gender roles. A critical reassessment of these perspectives in light of contemporary discussions on gender equality and inclusion underscores the need for a more equitable approach to educational philosophy.

Additionally, Locke's approach to political education and its role in shaping participatory and responsible citizens deserves critical consideration. While he advocates the idea that education should cultivate obedience to laws and authority, one could argue that today's political dynamics require a deeper and more critical understanding of the citizen's role in society. Contemporary discussions on civic education emphasize the importance of developing not only obedience but also critical thinking, active civic engagement, and the ability to constructively question power structures.

Another point worth analyzing is the influence of socioeconomic status on education, as Locke, despite defending the universal right to education, does not extensively explore the economic barriers that may hinder access. Educational equity is a central issue in contemporary debates, and Locke's work can be enriched by incorporating a deeper analysis of the economic disparities that directly impact the realization of the right to education.

Still, Locke's work offers an invaluable contribution to understanding education as a pillar of human development. His advocacy for intellectual freedom, moral development, and individuality in education continues to serve as a beacon for educators and thinkers interested in pursuing an educational approach that respects diversity and promotes the full potential of each individual.

In conclusion, *"Thoughts on Education"* by John Locke is a work that, despite its undeniable merits, does not escape critical reading in the contemporary context. Its lasting influence and the applicability of many of its principles are indisputable, but the work benefits from modern analysis to adapt to the challenges and complexities of today's society. By exploring its limitations, this critical review seeks to enrich the dialogue on the philosophy of education, recognizing Locke's continued relevance while inspiring new reflections and approaches in the pursuit of a more inclusive and meaningful education.

A Letter Concerning Toleration - 1689

John Locke's "A Letter Concerning Toleration" is a seminal work that transcends the barriers of time, resonating as an eloquent defense of religious tolerance and the separation between Church and State. Published in 1689, the work reflects the turbulent context of post-Reformation Europe, where tensions between different religious currents were palpable. Locke, one of the leading philosophers of the Enlightenment, constructs his argument with meticulousness, employing a logical and rational approach that characterizes his thought.

At its core, the work distills the idea that religious coercion is incompatible with individual freedom and harmful to societal well-being. It emphasizes that belief is an intimate matter, and the State should not usurp the role of individual conscience. One key point lies in the defense of the principle of religious tolerance grounded in human nature and the preservation of social peace. Locke argues that the diversity of beliefs is intrinsic to the human condition, requiring mutual respect and acceptance of differences for peaceful coexistence. This view, revolutionary for its time, outlines a path toward a more inclusive and harmonious society.

Locke's narrative incorporates a sharp critique of the absolutist claims of ecclesiastical and governmental authorities. His argument reflects a deep skepticism toward absolute power, suggesting that the separation between the religious and political spheres is not only desirable but essential to prevent abuses of power and preserve individual freedom. Throughout the work, Locke uses refined yet accessible language, demonstrating erudition without losing the ability to communicate his ideas clearly.

The persuasive strength of his arguments lies in his ability to articulate fundamental principles of liberty, equality, and tolerance within a robust philosophical context. The lasting influence of "A Letter Concerning Toleration" is manifested not only in the theoretical realm but also in the political transformations that shaped the foundations of modern democratic societies. Locke's thought reverberates in the ideas that underpinned the English Bill of Rights and later the United States Constitution.

His defense of religious liberty as an inalienable right of the individual contributed to the consolidation of principles that transcend temporal and geographical boundaries. The work, by its nature, also prompts reflections on cultural plurality and peaceful coexistence in increasingly diverse societies. By promoting religious tolerance, Locke anticipated contemporary debates about the coexistence of different creeds and belief systems. His vision resounds as a timeless appeal for the acceptance of diversity as a fundamental pillar in the construction of robust and inclusive societies.

Moreover, Locke's approach in "A Letter Concerning Toleration" later influenced political thinkers and philosophers who explored the relationship between State and religion. His emphasis on the separation between spheres, suggesting that temporal power should not interfere in religious matters and vice versa, fueled discussions on the secular nature of the State and the protection of individual freedoms in various contexts.

However, it cannot be ignored that Locke's work also faced criticisms and varying interpretations over the centuries. Some currents argue that his defense of tolerance, while crucial for his time, might be reinterpreted in light of contemporary complexities, especially when considering issues related to freedom of expression and the protection of minorities.

At the heart of "A Letter Concerning Toleration" lies Locke's fervent defense of freedom of conscience, a principle that echoes through the centuries as a strong voice against tyranny and the arbitrary imposition of beliefs. By grounding tolerance in the voluntary nature of the individual, Locke establishes a robust philosophical foundation for safeguarding fundamental freedoms, transcending temporal boundaries and offering a moral compass amid the vicissitudes of time.

The eloquence with which Locke intertwines theological, philosophical, and political arguments imparts to his work an intellectual richness that resists the test of time. His ability to articulate the importance of tolerance not only as a practical concession but as a moral imperative reveals a depth of thought that transcends the circumstantial debates of his time.

In a contemporary world marked by plurality and interconnection, Locke's words resonate as an invitation to mutual understanding and peaceful coexistence. Furthermore, "A Letter Concerning Toleration" significantly contributed to the evolution of discussions on the separation between Church and State. By arguing for the autonomy of the religious sphere in relation to temporal power, Locke anticipated fundamental principles that shaped democratic political systems around the globe. The emphasis on the autonomy of individual conscience as an intrinsic right influenced the development of a secular perspective, drawing clear lines between the functions of the State and the religious sphere.

However, one cannot overlook the fact that the practical application of Locke's principles has faced and continues to face complex challenges. The reconciliation between the tolerance advocated by Locke and the preservation of social and ethical values encounters contemporary dilemmas, such as the tensions between religious freedom and the protection of universal human rights. At the core of "A Letter Concerning Toleration," Locke highlights the urgent need for a society that recognizes the diversity of beliefs as an intrinsic expression of the human condition. His insightful argument is not limited to the theoretical sphere but resonates in everyday interactions and contemporary political struggles.

By conceiving tolerance not as a mere concession, but as a moral virtue that strengthens the foundations of peaceful coexistence, Locke outlines a vision that transcends the historical context, emerging as an ethical beacon for modern societies. The practical application of Locke's principles, however, is not without challenges and nuances. As societies evolve, debates about the limits of tolerance gain relevance, especially when confronted with complex ethical dilemmas. The protection of freedom of conscience, as proposed by Locke, must be balanced with the safeguarding of universal fundamental rights, thus preventing the instrumentalization of tolerance for the perpetuation of harmful practices or violations of human rights.

Locke's influence on the formation of political and legal structures is indisputable. His defense of the separation between religious authority and State power contributed to the consolidation of democratic systems that seek to preserve individual autonomy in the face of arbitrary impositions. "A Letter Concerning Toleration" not only outlines an ethical principle but also charts a path for the construction of societies where diversity is not only tolerated but celebrated as an enriching element of the human experience.

When critically analyzing Locke's work, it is essential to acknowledge the criticisms and divergent interpretations that have arisen over time. Some currents argue that his view could be interpreted as excessively centered on individual freedom, neglecting the complexities of social and cultural relations. Nevertheless, the strength of "A Letter Concerning Toleration" lies in its ability to trigger ongoing dialogues and profound reflections on the intersection of freedom, collective responsibility, and the construction of truly inclusive communities.

In sum, John Locke's work is a notable contribution to the philosophical and political canon. His defense of tolerance, permeated by language that is both accessible and erudite, endures as a guiding light for contemporary societies that seek a balance between preserving individual rights and promoting the common good. "A Letter Concerning Toleration" is, thus, a lasting testament to the human mind's ability to shape ideas that transcend the boundaries of time, rooting themselves in the heart of aspirations for justice and peaceful coexistence.

"Some Thoughts Concerning the Consequences of the Lowering of Interest and the Raising of the Value of Money" (1691)

"Some Thoughts Concerning the Consequences of the Lowering of Interest and the Raising of the Value of Money" by John Locke is a seminal work that stands out not only for the depth of its economic analysis but also for the author's insight into exploring the implications of the discovery of America in the context of the financial system of the time.

Locke, a renowned philosopher and political theorist of the 17th century, not only outlines the direct effects of changes in interest rates and the value of money but also sheds light on the broader dynamics that permeate the emerging economy of the time. The author begins his analysis by contextualizing the impact of the discovery of America, recognizing it as an event of transcendental magnitude that reverberated across various spheres of society.

Locke argues that this discovery influenced not only trade and the availability of resources but also shaped economic and financial structures, triggering a process of reassessment of Europe's monetary practices. His careful and meticulous approach resonates with the scholarship characteristic of his work.

In exploring the implications of the discovery of America on interest rates, Locke offers a penetrating analysis of the complexities involving the relationship between the influx of gold and silver and loan dynamics. He maintains that the increased availability of these precious metals, as a result of exploration in the Americas, triggered a series of changes in interest rates. Locke argues that the abundance of gold and silver led to a reduction in interest rates, fundamentally altering lending and investment practices.

Furthermore, the author thoroughly explores the ramifications of the increased value of money, resulting from the influx of precious metals from the newly discovered colonies. Locke discusses how this elevation of the value of money affected internal and external prices, as well as trade relations between nations. His insightful economic analysis transcends the limitations of his time, providing a deep understanding of the interconnections between economic changes and historical events.

In terms of style, Locke's prose exhibits a clarity that reflects his ability to communicate complex ideas in an accessible manner. His academic language, rich in specific terminology, contributes to the solidity of his argument, while his capacity to articulate economic concepts in a comprehensible way stands out as a distinctive mark of his intellectual mastery.

John Locke's work becomes even more complex and enriching as it addresses the philosophical and ethical repercussions of the economic transformations brought about by the discovery of America. Locke does not limit himself to a merely quantitative analysis but extends his critical eye to the underlying ethical issues surrounding changes in the financial system. He questions how such alterations affect the distribution of wealth, emphasizing the importance of an ethical approach in considering the social consequences of these changes.

The intersection of the economic and the ethical in Locke's work is particularly evident in his reflection on property. The author explores how economic transformations impact the notion of property, discussing how the abundance of precious metals from the Americas influences the accumulation of wealth and, by extension, the social structure. Locke argues that the change in economic dynamics calls for a reassessment of traditional conceptions of property, highlighting the need for an ethical analysis that takes into account not only individual interests but also the common good.

Locke's insight is evident in how he anticipates and addresses contemporary issues related to economic globalization. His reflections on the impact of the discovery of America echo in modern discussions about the role of emerging nations in the global scene. Locke provides a pioneering viewpoint, exploring the implications of an interconnected economy, highlighting the challenges and opportunities that arise when economic borders expand.

Moreover, Locke's analysis of the relationship between money and trade not only provides an in-depth understanding of the historical context but also serves as a theoretical foundation for contemporary discussions on monetary policies and their implications. Locke's ability to anticipate enduring economic dynamics demonstrates not only his intellectual mastery but also the timelessness of his contributions to economic thought.

The interdisciplinary aspect of Locke's work becomes even more evident in the connection between his economic ideas and his foundational political principles. His reflection on property as a natural and inalienable right serves as a starting point for his future elaborations on political theory, establishing a conceptual basis that permeates his subsequent works. This shows the intrinsic cohesion between the different domains of Locke's thought, where economic analysis organically converges with his political and ethical considerations.

The exploration of the concept of labor as the foundation of economic value is a notable aspect of Locke's analysis. The author argues that true value resides in human labor, a view that, in addition to influencing his economic considerations, permeates his political conceptions. The idea that labor is the legitimate source of property lays the groundwork for Locke's theory of natural rights and property, outlining an intrinsic connection between the economic and political spheres of his thought.

Locke's focus on the relationship between precious metals and money also reveals a sophisticated understanding of the nuances of the financial system. He not only examines the direct implications of this relationship but also recognizes its broader ramifications for economic and social stability. The issue of inflation, for example, is addressed with a depth that transcends the immediacy of the historical context, highlighting Locke's ability to anticipate economic concerns that resonate even today.

Even more impressive is Locke's ability to articulate a vision of society grounded in reason and the social contract, a vision that would become central to many subsequent political theories. By discussing the nature of property, he not only offers insights into economic changes but also lays the foundations for a broader understanding of social and political organization. His emphasis on the need for limited government and respect for individual rights shapes a vision of society that transcends economic vicissitudes.

The eclectic and carefully crafted language of Locke, which permeates his entire work, contributes to the strength of his arguments. His ability to employ technical terminology in an accessible manner demonstrates not only his intellectual prowess but also his intention to communicate his ideas to a diverse audience. This aspect of his writing makes the work not only a valuable academic contribution but also an accessible source of understanding for readers with varying levels of familiarity with economic and political theory.

In summary, "Some Thoughts Concerning the Consequences of the Lowering of Interest and the Raising of the Value of Money" by John Locke not only stands out as a seminal work in economic thought but also as a document that transcends the boundaries between economics, politics, and ethics. Locke's ability to connect these domains in a coherent and enlightening way not only enriches the understanding of his time but also provides a robust foundation for contemporary analyses, thereby reinforcing the timelessness and relevance of his intellectual contribution.

"A Project for a New Coin" (Some Considerations of the Consequences of the Lowering of Interest and the Raising of the Value of Money) - 1691

"A Project for a New Coin," originally titled "Some Considerations of the Consequences of the Lowering of Interest and the Raising of the Value of Money," is a seminal work written by John Locke in the late 17th century. This work, which falls under the scope of monetary and economic theory, reflects Locke's deep reflections on the effects of changes in interest rates and the value of money on the economy of his time.

At the heart of Locke's argument lies the interdependence between interest rates and the intrinsic value of money. The author proposes a careful view of the consequences associated with the reduction of interest rates and the appreciation of money, shedding light on the intricate mechanisms that shape the economic fabric. Locke, with his characteristic erudition, highlights the complexity of these variables and emphasizes the need for a balanced approach in financial management.

Locke's approach is marked by a rigorous theoretical grounding, anchored in fundamental economic principles. His meticulous analysis of the ramifications of changes in interest rates reveals a keen understanding of economic dynamics. The author contextualizes his proposals within the economic and political climate of the time, providing a comprehensive view of the forces that drive the fluctuation of interest rates and the value of money.

Furthermore, Locke's work transcends the boundaries of his time, offering insights relevant to contemporary economic discussions. The author's ability to anticipate the implications of monetary policies is notable, and his considerations continue to resonate in modern economic debates. The text echoes with an acuity that transcends the temporal barrier, establishing itself as an essential reference for scholars and practitioners of economics.

Regarding literary form, Locke displays an eloquence that elevates his work to a level beyond the merely technical. His fluid and accessible prose not only facilitates the understanding of economic complexities but also adds an attractive layer to the reading. Locke's ability to articulate arguments clearly and persuasively contributes to the ongoing relevance of his work in the academic sphere.

Locke's proposal for a new coin does not limit itself to a static analysis of monetary relations but encompasses a dynamic view of the interaction between various economic agents. The author, when discussing the implications of lowering interest rates, emphasizes not only the immediate effects on investments and consumption but also the influence of such changes on the expectations of economic agents.

Locke envisions the economy as an interconnected system, where the decisions of one sector reverberate throughout the economic fabric, resulting in consequences that go beyond the financial realm. One of the most notable aspects of Locke's work lies in his insight into the relationship between monetary policies and economic stability. The author does not merely describe changes in interest rates but also weaves considerations about the potential imbalances that may arise.

Locke warns of the risks of financial instability and inflation, emphasizing the importance of a balanced approach in conducting monetary policies. His cautious view reflects a deep understanding of the nuances inherent in economic management. Moreover, Locke's work reveals a constant concern for equity and social justice. When exploring the effects of changes in interest rates, the author not only focuses on macroeconomic aspects but also examines the implications for different strata of society.

His approach incorporates a social awareness, seeking to balance economic considerations with ethical concerns. This holistic approach adds an ethical dimension to the analysis of monetary policies, distinguishing Locke's work in a field often dominated by strictly technical approaches. Locke's approach in "A Project for a New Coin" reveals not only a sharp understanding of economic mechanisms but also an awareness of the importance of institutional stability.

He argues that abrupt changes in interest rates and the value of money can trigger disruptive effects not only in the economic sphere but also on the foundations of society. Locke, in his analysis, seems to anticipate the need for careful management of monetary policies to preserve not only economic stability but also social cohesion.

Locke's perspective on the relationship between interest rates and economic activity is rooted in a long-term view. He recognizes that fluctuations in interest rates have implications that extend over time, affecting not only the current generation but also future ones. This temporal consideration adds an intergenerational responsibility dimension to Locke's analysis, highlighting his comprehensive vision of the impact of monetary policies on the continuity and stability of societies.

As for the methodology employed by Locke, it is clear that his approach is grounded in a careful synthesis of theory and empirical observation. The author does not limit himself to abstract speculations but bases his conclusions on a solid analysis of the economic conditions of his time. His ability to balance theoretical principles with practical reality strengthens the credibility of his work and contributes to its lasting relevance.

Moreover, the clarity and coherence of Locke's argumentation are remarkable. He weaves a complex narrative in an accessible way, making his insights available to a broad audience. This expository quality not only facilitates the understanding of intricate economic concepts but also extends the reach of his influence, allowing his ideas to transcend the boundaries of academia.

However, it is crucial to acknowledge that, despite Locke's notable contribution, the work is not immune to criticism. Some contemporary analyses question the direct applicability of his proposals in radically different economic contexts. Furthermore, subsequent developments in economic theory may provide additional perspectives on the topics addressed by Locke.

In summary, John Locke's "A Project for a New Coin" represents not only a profound analysis of the economic complexities of his time but also a solid foundation for understanding the interactions between monetary policies, social stability, and temporality. The work stands out for its balanced approach, long-term perspective, and expository clarity, consolidating Locke's position as a prominent figure in the history of economic thought.

Constitution of Carolina – 1669

John Locke's *Constitution of Carolina* is a seminal work in the fields of political theory and philosophy of law, representing a significant contribution to 17th-century Enlightenment thought. In this text, Locke outlines his vision for the ideal constitutional structure for the colony of Carolina, offering a sophisticated synthesis of his fundamental philosophical principles. The heart of the work lies in Locke's contractualist perspective, where political authority is legitimized by the consent of the governed.

The author seeks to establish a social contract aimed at ensuring the protection of individuals' natural rights, such as life, liberty, and property. The importance of a governmental structure intrinsically linked to the will of the people is emphasized, thus highlighting the essential nature of democratic representation. The language used by Locke is characterized by clarity and precision, qualities that contribute to the accessibility of the text. His ability to articulate complex arguments in an understandable way is crucial for the effective dissemination of his ideas.

A critical analysis of the *Constitution of Carolina* highlights the lasting influence of Locke's thought on modern political theory. Concepts such as the separation of powers and the limitation of governmental power have played a significant role in the formation of constitutional systems worldwide. However, it is imperative to recognize that the historical context of 17th-century Carolina may limit the direct applicability of certain propositions from Locke today.

Furthermore, Locke's emphasis on the protection of property may generate contemporary criticisms, especially when considering the growing concerns about equity and social justice. A literal application of his principles in contemporary contexts requires careful analysis and adaptation to ensure a more just and egalitarian society. Moreover, it is essential to examine Locke's approach to freedom and religious tolerance, an aspect that permeates his work and acquires particular relevance in societies characterized by cultural and religious diversity.

Locke advocates for the freedom of conscience, defending the separation between political power and individual religious convictions. His progressive view in this regard, marked by religious tolerance, establishes a paradigm for peaceful coexistence in pluralistic societies and resonates in contemporary debates on religious freedom. However, critics point to possible limitations in the practical application of these principles, noting that, in his specific formulation for Carolina, Locke maintained some reservations about extending this tolerance to groups considered "intolerant."

This apparent ambiguity in Locke's position highlights the inherent complexity of reconciling theory with the practical realities of governance. Another critical point of discussion is Locke's emphasis on property as a fundamental right. While the protection of property is undeniably central to his work, some contemporary interpretations raise questions about how this emphasis may perpetuate socioeconomic inequalities.

The evolution of modern societies has brought forth significant challenges related to the equitable distribution of resources and the protection of the most vulnerable, challenges that may require adjustments to Locke's conceptions to fit the ethical and moral demands of contemporary times. Additionally, the structure proposed by Locke for Carolina reveals a central concern for stability and order, reflecting his conviction that an effective government must ensure the security of citizens and the preservation of property.

The separation of powers, one of the fundamental pillars of Locke's theory, is outlined as a crucial mechanism to avoid the excessive concentration of authority and to prevent potential abuses of power by the government. However, the practical implementation of this theory requires careful consideration of contextual nuances, taking into account the peculiarities of the society it is intended for. Locke's reverence for the principles of the state of nature and the social contract also raises reflections on the intrinsic nature of the human condition.

While some praise his optimistic view of the human capacity for reason and cooperation, others question the adequacy of these assumptions given the complexities inherent in human nature. The criticism may lie in the idea that the state of nature is conceived in an excessively idealized manner, overlooking the darker and less rational dimensions of human behavior that sometimes emerge in challenging social contexts.

Regarding the practical application of his ideas, the *Constitution of Carolina* serves as a starting point for contemporary discussions on the formation and adaptation of legal and political systems. As societies face pressing issues related to justice, equality, and individual rights, Locke's work encourages modern interpreters to consider how his principles can be integrated and reinterpreted to address the ethical challenges of the 21st century.

Another element that deserves critical attention in Locke's work is the question of civic participation and access to the political process. While his defense of democratic representation was revolutionary in his time, some contemporary analyses argue that the political structures proposed by Locke may not have adequately addressed inclusivity and equity in the decision-making process.

Reflecting on the extent of citizens' involvement in the formation of laws and policies, especially in an increasingly globalized world, offers an opportunity to reexamine the conceptual foundations of democracy proposed by Locke. The historical contextualization of the *Constitution of Carolina* also sheds light on the complexities inherent in Locke's political thought.

The 17th century witnessed a series of social, economic, and political transformations, and Carolina was not immune to these changes. The specific demands of the colonial environment, with its unique dynamics, influenced Locke's formulations in ways that may not be directly translatable to other temporal or geographical contexts. Moreover, the intersection of Locke's political theory with his views on education and civic formation deserves further analysis.

The author's emphasis on the importance of public instruction and educational development for the preservation of liberty highlights a central concern with the formation of virtuous and informed citizens. However, the implications of this perspective for the diversity of educational experiences and for equity in access to education warrant consideration in light of contemporary realities. Another crucial aspect is Locke's approach to the nature of political power and its legitimization.

The emphasis on the need for consent and the limitation of governmental power is undoubtedly an advance in the protection of individual rights. However, contemporary criticisms may focus on the adequacy of these principles in dealing with global challenges and transnational issues that transcend national borders, raising questions about the effectiveness of such structures in the face of complex dilemmas such as climate change, mass migration, and global inequality.

The lasting relevance of the *Constitution of Carolina* also stimulates reflections on the application of Locke's ideas in contexts that are not only geographical but also cultural. The universality of his principles, often celebrated, can be critically examined in light of cultural diversity and different legal traditions.

Cultural and historical contextualization thus becomes a key piece in the contemporary interpretation of Locke's proposals, recognizing the nuances and multiplicity of perspectives that permeate modern societies. Furthermore, the intersection of Locke's political theory with issues of gender and identity deserves further in-depth analysis.

The *Constitution of Carolina* can be seen as a product of its time, reflecting prevailing conceptions of gender roles and social relations. Contemporary criticism may focus on the need to reinterpret and expand Locke's ideas to encompass the complexities of contemporary experiences and identities, ensuring a more inclusive and equitable approach. Ultimately, the critical review of the *Constitution of Carolina* highlights not only the intellectual grandeur of John Locke but also calls scholars to engage in ongoing dialogues about the adaptation and application of the fundamental ideas of the work in light of the ethical, social, and political challenges of the 21st century. The ability to question, reinterpret, and evolve these principles is key to keeping the relevance of this seminal work alive in the contemporary landscape.

A Second Letter Concerning Toleration (1690)

John Locke's *A Second Letter Concerning Toleration* is a fundamental work that stands out in the philosophical landscape of the 17th century, offering a compelling and meticulous defense of religious tolerance. Locke, one of the leading thinkers of the Enlightenment, develops his argument with insight, using clear and rational language, key characteristics of his philosophical approach.

The core of the work lies in the defense of religious freedom as a fundamental pillar of a just and equitable society. Locke seeks to ground his position in reason, arguing that coercion in religious matters is counterproductive and, rather than promoting truth, generates conflicts and dissensions that harm social peace. The author argues that the government should refrain from imposing a specific religion, allowing citizens to practice their beliefs according to their conscience.

Locke highlights the crucial distinction between the religious and civil spheres, emphasizing that the authority of the state should be limited to temporal matters, while the spiritual sphere should be governed by individual freedom. Locke employs a rationalist approach, appealing to the human ability to discern between right and wrong, arguing that coercion does not lead to true conviction but only to superficial conformity.

Locke's ability to articulate his ideas logically and coherently is evident throughout the work. He addresses potential objections meticulously, anticipating criticisms and refuting opposing arguments with scholarship that shows his deep understanding of the theological and political debates of his time. His defense of tolerance is not just a matter of abstract principles, but is based on a practical analysis of the social and political dynamics.

Locke's approach to religious tolerance is deeply rooted in his optimistic view of human nature. He believes in individuals' capacity to use their reason to seek truth, asserting that coercion leads only to outward obedience without promoting genuine religious conviction. This trust in human rationality as a guide for moral conduct reflects Enlightenment thought, where the light of reason is seen as a beacon for human progress.

In exploring the relationship between religion and politics, Locke establishes a delicate balance between religious freedom and the need to maintain civil order. He argues that the state should not interfere in matters of faith but reserves the right to intervene when civil peace is threatened. This subtle distinction between the religious and civil spheres outlines the limits of government authority, protecting individual freedom without compromising social stability.

The contemporary relevance of Locke's work is remarkable, as his reflections on tolerance resonate in increasingly diverse and pluralistic societies. His ideas continue to challenge authoritarian and fundamentalist conceptions, promoting the notion that peaceful coexistence is possible even amidst profound differences in religious beliefs.

It is crucial to note that Locke does not propose a relativist view that equates all beliefs, but instead defends the freedom of each individual to follow their conscience. His defense of tolerance is not merely a theoretical issue, but also a pragmatic response to the sectarian conflicts that plagued 17th-century Europe. His balanced approach reflects a sophisticated understanding of social and political dynamics, recognizing the importance of diversity while seeking to preserve social cohesion.

Locke's insight into religious tolerance is also evident in how he incorporates historical and theological elements into his argument. By contextualizing his defense within the framework of the sectarian tensions of the 17th century, Locke highlights the urgency of finding common ground that allows peaceful coexistence among different religious groups. His analysis of religious wars and persecution is grounded in a deep understanding of historical complexities, providing a solid foundation for his propositions.

The influence of Locke's ideas extends beyond the theoretical realm and into political practice. His call for tolerance as an essential principle for social stability and human development had significant implications for discussions on the separation of church and state. Locke's understanding that religious coercion is counterproductive to the flourishing of truth and peaceful coexistence resonates in the modern conception of individual rights and fundamental freedoms.

Another notable aspect of Locke's work is his insistence on the importance of equal religious rights for all communities, regardless of their majority or minority status. This emphasis on equality reflects not only a vision of justice but also a subtle understanding of the power dynamics that can emerge in pluralistic societies. Locke anticipates the need to protect religious minorities, recognizing that true freedom can only exist when extended to all, regardless of their position in the social majority.

John Locke's *A Second Letter Concerning Toleration* is a philosophical gem that transcends temporal boundaries, still resonating in discussions about religious freedom and peaceful coexistence. Locke, a prominent Enlightenment thinker, eloquently challenges the concept of religious coercion and state intervention, providing a robust defense of tolerance as an essential foundation for social harmony.

Locke's distinctive ability to harmonize reason with theological and historical complexities gives his argument unparalleled solidity. His analysis of religious wars and persecutions, grounded in a keen understanding of sociopolitical dynamics, reveals not only his scholarship but also his awareness of the urgency of addressing the sectarian conflicts that marked his time.

Locke's pragmatic influence is evident in the way his ideas transcend the realm of philosophical theories to shape political practice. His defense of the separation of church and state and his insistence on equal religious rights for all communities foreshadow modern debates on individual rights and fundamental freedoms. Locke not only delineates a theoretical argument but also offers a practical guide for building societies that value belief diversity without sacrificing social cohesion.

By highlighting the importance of equal religious rights for minorities, Locke not only reveals his vision of justice but also understands the need to protect the most vulnerable groups in a pluralistic society. His balanced approach emphasizes not only individual freedom but also recognizes the state's responsibilities in ensuring civil peace, thus establishing a delicate balance between the religious and civil spheres.

In summary, *A Second Letter Concerning Toleration* is more than an eloquent defense of tolerance; it is a masterful treatise that anchors the principles of religious freedom in a robust and multifaceted analysis. Locke's work continues to play a crucial role in contemporary debates, providing a lasting legacy that transcends temporal boundaries and continues to illuminate discussions on the relationship between faith, government, and society.

"Civil Government" (1680)

John Locke's *"Civil Government"* is a seminal work that played a crucial role in shaping modern political ideas. Originally published in 1689, the work stands out as a key piece in the development of Enlightenment thought, outlining the foundations of the social contract and significantly influencing subsequent political theories.

Locke begins his work by exploring the nature of the state of nature, a fundamental concept in his political philosophy. He argues that, in the state of nature, men have natural rights, such as life, liberty, and property, but also acknowledges the inherent limitations of this state, such as the lack of a common authority to resolve disputes. This detailed analysis of the state of nature serves as the starting point for his theory of the social contract.

Introducing the idea of the social contract, Locke proposes that individuals, in seeking protection for their natural rights, consent to form a government. This transition from the state of nature to the civil state is marked by a tacit agreement between rulers and the ruled, establishing the legitimacy of political power. Locke's contractual approach significantly influenced later thinkers, such as Rousseau and Kant.

Throughout his work, Locke presents a careful analysis of the separation of powers, a principle that would later become a cornerstone of modern political theory. By advocating for the division of powers into legislative, executive, and judicial branches, he seeks to prevent abuse of authority and ensure the preservation of individual rights. This government structure, masterfully outlined by Locke, directly influenced the framers of the United States Constitution.

Locke's emphasis on the protection of property as an inalienable natural right also played a central role in shaping subsequent political thought. The notion of property extends beyond the possession of tangible goods, encompassing individual rights and autonomy. This perspective influenced debates on individual freedom and the limits of state power throughout history.

In addition to his notable contribution to political theory, Locke's *"Civil Government"* stands out for its passionate defense of individual rights and freedom. Locke believes that government should be the guardian of natural rights, and any political authority that violates these rights loses its legitimacy. This perspective resonates significantly in contemporary debates on the relationship between the individual and the state, influencing movements that seek to protect civil rights and individual freedoms.

One of the distinctive features of the work is its pragmatic approach to resistance against tyrannical political power. Locke argues that, if a ruler violates the fundamental principles of the social contract by usurping individuals' liberty and property, they have the right—and even the duty—to resist such authority. This subtly introduces the idea of a government limited by the consent of the governed, an idea that would become central to modern democratic movements.

Moreover, Locke's influence extends beyond the political sphere, reaching the realm of moral philosophy. His theory of identity and knowledge formation through experience, known as empiricism, challenges previous conceptions and lays the foundation for the later development of epistemology. This interconnectedness between his political and epistemological philosophy highlights the breadth of Locke's thought and his multifaceted contribution to the philosophical canon.

Throughout the work, Locke also addresses the issue of religious tolerance, advocating for the separation of church and state. His defense of the right to religious freedom and tolerance as crucial components of peaceful coexistence influenced the evolution of pluralistic and democratic societies. This tolerant vision is a distinctive feature of the work, promoting an inclusive understanding of diverse beliefs and perspectives in the public sphere.

In addition to its notable influence in political and philosophical fields, Locke's *"Civil Government"* extends its impact to the legal domain, providing conceptual foundations for the development of natural rights theory and its integration into legal frameworks. By establishing the inalienable rights of life, liberty, and property, Locke sows the seeds of a legal approach that recognizes the inviolability of these rights as guiding principles in the formulation and interpretation of laws.

The intersection between Locke's political theory and legal theory is particularly evident in his conception of property as a fundamental right. Locke argues that property is acquired through labor and the mixing of labor with nature, providing a solid justification for private property rights. This notion of property as an extension of individual labor permeates not only his political reflections but also establishes fertile ground for discussions on distributive justice and contractual relations in the legal realm.

Locke's work also echoes in contemporary debates about the legitimacy of power and the state's responsibility in protecting citizens. His emphasis on limiting governmental power to preserve individuals' natural rights resonates in discussions about the rule of law and the need for a legal structure that ensures equality before the law. The notion that government should be a means of protecting individual rights, rather than an entity that subjugates them, remains a crucial consideration in modern jurisprudence.

Furthermore, Locke's approach to education and the formation of knowledge, linking them to empirical experience, triggered reflections that transcended the philosophical domain to influence pedagogy and educational policies. His defense of the human mind as a "blank slate" shaped by experience and observation resonates in contemporary theories about learning and cognitive development.

In conclusion, John Locke's *"Civil Government"* not only provides a robust framework for political theory but also leaves a lasting legacy in the legal and educational spheres. The work continues to be an essential reference for thinkers, jurists, and educators, standing out as a rich and multifaceted source that transcends disciplinary boundaries and enriches intellectual dialogue across various fields of knowledge.

"Reasonableness of Christianity" (1695)

John Locke's *Reasonableness of Christianity* is a masterful work that stands out for its analytical and critical approach to the Christian faith. Published at the end of the 17th century, the book reflects not only the author's scholarship but also the intellectual atmosphere of the time, marked by the transition from medieval thought to modernity.

The book fits within the context of the Enlightenment, presenting a view that seeks to reconcile reason with the fundamental principles of Christianity. One of the distinguishing features of Locke's work is his empirical and rational approach to religion. Instead of relying strictly on dogmatic authority, the author proposes a careful analysis of sacred texts, aiming to identify the essential principles that are reasonable and accessible to the human mind.

This critical stance, though bold for its time, represents a significant effort to harmonize faith with reason, establishing a dialogue between the religious sphere and the emerging Enlightenment thought. Locke argues that the essence of Christianity is understandable by human reason and that dogmas should be interpreted in light of rationality. He emphasizes the importance of religious tolerance, rejecting the coercive imposition of beliefs and advocating for freedom of conscience.

This approach had a significant influence on the subsequent development of political and religious thought, contributing to the construction of a more pluralistic society that respects individual differences. However, the work is not without its critics. Some argue that Locke's approach could be interpreted as an attempt to domesticate faith, subjecting it excessively to human reason.

The issue of interpreting sacred texts remains complex, and the quest for universal reasonableness may, in some cases, seem oversimplified in light of the richness and diversity of religious traditions. Furthermore, Locke's work not only addresses the reconciliation between reason and faith but also delves into fundamental theological questions that permeate Christianity.

The author explores the nature of God, redemption, and morality, proposing interpretations that seek to reconcile divine revelation with logical principles accessible to the human mind. In doing so, Locke not only challenges contemporary orthodoxies but also establishes the foundations for a theological reflection that transcends confessional boundaries.

Locke's analysis of the relationship between divine will and human freedom is particularly noteworthy. His approach offers a balanced view that recognizes God's sovereignty without compromising the moral autonomy of the human being. The Lockean notion that reason is an essential tool for understanding divine purposes marks a significant break from traditional views of the time, which often emphasized unquestionable submission to religious authority.

Another relevant aspect is the influence of the political and social context on Locke's formulation of ideas. The author lived in a period marked by religious conflicts and political tensions, elements that inevitably shaped his view of the need for a reasonable and tolerant faith as a foundation for peaceful coexistence.

Locke's approach transcends the theological realm, also engaging intrinsically with the social challenges of his time. However, it must be acknowledged that Locke's work is not free from ambiguities. The attempt to reconcile reason and faith can, at times, seem simplistic in the face of the inherent complexity of theological issues.

The universality of reasonableness proposed by Locke may be questioned, as different religious traditions hold distinct interpretations of what constitutes reasonable faith. Moreover, in examining Locke's work, it is essential to consider the broader context of the Enlightenment, an intellectual movement that resonated across Europe in the 17th century.

Reasonableness of Christianity emerges as a unique piece in this context, as Locke not only embraces Enlightenment ideals of reason, liberty, and tolerance but also applies them to the religious sphere. His defense of the autonomy of reason in interpreting Christian principles aligns with the broader quest for a grounded and logical understanding of all aspects of human existence.

Another fascinating aspect of the work lies in the way Locke articulates his vision of the relationship between faith and morality. The author proposes a Christian ethics that is not only grounded in divine revelation but also finds resonance in human conscience and rational virtues. This perspective, which highlights the universality of ethical principles, transcends denominational boundaries, offering a common foundation for Christian ethics that can engage with different moral traditions.

At the same time, it is crucial to address the criticisms Locke's work has received over the centuries. Some theological currents argue that his emphasis on reason as a guide to interpreting sacred texts may lead to a dilution of the authenticity of faith. The complexity of theological issues often challenges simplification attempts, and the appeal to reason may, in some cases, be seen as an excessive reduction of the spiritual depth inherent in the religious experience.

Ultimately, *Reasonableness of Christianity* by John Locke is a work that transcends the boundaries of its time, presenting a unique approach to the reconciliation of reason and faith. Its legacy resonates in contemporary discussions about the relationship between religion, philosophy, and society, inspiring critical reflections on the nature of belief and the need for tolerance in a world characterized by diverse perspectives. Locke, by exploring the paths of reason applied to theology, left a lasting impact that continues to influence religious and philosophical thought to this day.

"Human Reason" - 1690

John Locke's *Human Reason* is a work that stands out as a cornerstone in 17th-century Enlightenment thought. Locke, an English empiricist philosopher, presents a meticulous analysis of the nature and limits of human reason, exploring fundamental issues that echo throughout the history of philosophy.

His text demonstrates a unique ability to articulate complex ideas in an accessible manner, contributing to the breadth of his influence on the development of Western thought. At the core of the work, Locke examines the origin and extent of human knowledge, advocating the thesis that the human mind is a "tabula rasa" – a blank slate upon which sensory experiences shape understanding. This innovative epistemological approach challenges the predominant innate conceptions of the time, marking a paradigm shift that reverberates in subsequent philosophies.

Grounded in his theory of the mind, Locke explores the nature of government and politics in his work, emphasizing the importance of preserving individual natural rights. His political treatise, especially reflected in *Two Treatises of Government*, lays the foundation for modern liberal thought, asserting that government should derive its power from the consent of the governed.

However, the work is not without criticism. Some philosophical schools contest Locke's empirical view, arguing that it underestimates the importance of innate mental faculties. Additionally, ethical issues related to slavery and colonization, present in Locke's historical context, have sparked contemporary debates about the validity of his ideas in light of current values.

In the ethical realm, Locke delves into the complexities of morality by exploring the concept of natural rights, outlining a vision that would become essential for the foundation of democratic political systems. His defense of private property as a natural right, for example, lays the groundwork for a modern understanding of economic and social principles, underpinning subsequent arguments on individual liberty and equality.

Nevertheless, it is imperative to recognize that Locke's work is not immune to contemporary criticism. Ambiguities and gaps in his theory, particularly regarding the specific origin of natural rights, have sparked academic debates within philosophical and political circles. Furthermore, questions about the universality of his principles across diverse cultural contexts are relevant, given that the indiscriminate application of ideas formulated in a specific time period may overlook the multiplicity of ethical and cultural perspectives.

Another critical point of analysis focuses on Locke's relationship with religious issues. Although often associated with advocating for religious tolerance, especially in his *Letter Concerning Toleration*, the exact interpretation of his religious views and their influence on his political thinking remains a subject of controversy. The tension between reason and faith, intrinsically expressed in his work, adds layers of complexity to the understanding of Locke as an emblematic figure of the Enlightenment.

In the contemporary context, *Human Reason* continues to be the subject of study and analysis across various disciplines, from philosophy to political science. Its relevance persists not only due to the depth of the issues it addresses but also because of the adaptability and dialogue of its ideas with the ethical challenges and dilemmas of modern society. For a more comprehensive appreciation of Locke's work, it is crucial to examine its impact on the development of political theory and modern philosophy.

Human Reason is undoubtedly a seminal document that contributed to the paradigm shift in political thought, influencing subsequent thinkers such as Montesquieu and the founders of the United States. Locke's emphasis on popular sovereignty and the social contract as the legitimate basis for government provided a theoretical framework that reverberated in the conception of democracy and individual rights.

However, the paradoxical nature of Locke's influence is revealed when exploring the implications of his ideas on colonialism and slavery during his time. The relationship between his theories of liberty and private property and the exploitation of land and people raises significant ethical questions. This dichotomy presents substantial challenges for contemporary thought, prompting a critical analysis of the inherent contradictions in the ideas that shaped the foundations of liberal thought.

Furthermore, Locke's articulation of the separation between legislative and executive powers, advocating for the principle of the division of powers, directly influenced the formation of modern political systems. This division of powers is viewed as an essential safeguard against authoritarianism, but again, the practical application of these ideas raises questions about the effectiveness of these mechanisms in dealing with contemporary governance and justice challenges.

Regarding Locke's influence on constitutional theory, his ideas permeate discussions on the role of the social contract in the formation of legitimate governments. The principle of consent of the governed as the basis for political authority, as outlined by Locke, echoes in modern constitutions, but varied interpretations of this consent raise fundamental questions about the effective and informed participation of citizens in political decisions.

Additionally, Locke's impact extends to the field of education, with his reflections on the mind as a "blank slate" shaped by experience. The influence of this view on pedagogy and educational theories is notable, fueling debates on teaching methods, the role of the educator, and cognitive development.

In summary, *Human Reason* by John Locke, encompassing such broad themes as epistemology, politics, and ethics, continues to challenge intellectuals to explore and interpret its complexities. The resonance of his ideas transcends temporal boundaries, establishing Locke as a philosopher whose work endures as a beacon for understanding the human condition and social organization.

"Economic Writings"

John Locke's *Economic Writings* is a seminal work that stands out in the canon of classical economic theory. Locke, one of the foundational philosophers of the Enlightenment Era, presents a meticulous and innovative analysis of economic relations, shaping the foundations for subsequent thought on political economy.

This comprehensive compendium is a compilation of his substantial contributions on economic topics, providing a thorough and deeply articulated view of the forces driving the functioning of societies. A notable aspect of Locke's work is his empirically grounded approach to understanding the economic system. Unlike many of his contemporaries, Locke advocates for careful observation and evidence-based analysis to understand economic dynamics. This approach, deeply rooted in the emerging scientific method of the time, provides his work with a solid foundation and lasting relevance.

The author unfolds his ideas through extensive treatises, in which he explores topics ranging from the nature of property to the role of government in economic regulation. His defense of private property as the cornerstone of economic development and individual freedom resonates as a profound reflection on the principles that permeate modern societies. Locke weaves an intricate argumentative tapestry, connecting philosophical, political, and economic elements to form a comprehensive view of the market's role in social organization.

Moreover, Locke offers an insightful analysis of government influence on the economy. His balanced view on state intervention reflects a subtle understanding of the complexities inherent in economic management. By emphasizing the need for an effective government, he proposes clear limits to avoid excesses that might harm individual freedom and economic progress.

The resilience and relevance of Locke's contributions to economic theory are evident in the depth of his analysis on wealth distribution and the nature of labor. In his exploration of the labor theory of value, Locke presents a robust view on how labor is the foundation of economic value creation. His perspective influenced later thinkers, contributing to the development of classical economic theories that highlight the importance of labor in wealth formation and structuring social relations.

In examining international relations and foreign trade, Locke stands out for his insightful understanding of the mutual benefits derived from trade. In a period when nations were beginning to expand through global trade routes, his ideas on economic interdependence and trade gains are remarkably visionary. The interconnection of his economic analyses with international political issues demonstrates a holistic and integrated approach, marking Locke as a precursor to globalized economic thought.

Another crucial point in the work is Locke's approach to currency and its role in the economy. He offers a detailed analysis of the nature of money, arguing that its value is not inherent but derived from agreement and consent. This perspective, though it has been the subject of subsequent debate, contributed to contemporary understanding of monetary dynamics and the evolution of monetary theories over time.

It is imperative to consider Locke's influence on the development of liberal economic ideas that shaped modern democracies. His conceptions of property, liberty, and the limits of governmental power have been incorporated into the philosophical and political foundations that inform many contemporary social structures. Locke, thus, not only contributed to the economic sphere but also played a significant role in shaping the ideological bases of democratic societies.

Among Locke's most notable contributions is his pioneering approach to the idea of capital accumulation. In *Economic Writings*, he examines the mechanisms by which private property and individual labor intertwine to generate wealth, drawing parallels between economic activity and social development. His emphasis on the importance of labor as the primary source of value, combined with his defense of private property as a driver of productivity, significantly influenced later theories on capitalism and wealth formation.

By delving into the complexities of Locke's theory, one can discern his subtle approach to the ethical issues that permeate the economic sphere. Locke seeks to reconcile moral principles with economic dynamics, exploring the role of fair trade and equity in the distribution of resources. This integration of ethical considerations into economic analysis is a distinctive aspect of his work, which resonates beyond his time, echoing in contemporary debates on social responsibility and business ethics.

In the context of 17th-century political-economic thought, Locke emerges as a pioneering advocate for the idea that government should be a facilitating agent of economic development. His balanced approach to state intervention, advocating for the need for an effective government without disregarding the dangers of excessive governmental intrusion, resonates particularly in times when the relationship between the state and the economy remains a central issue in political and academic discussions.

However, it is vital to recognize that the historical context in which Locke wrote also shaped his perspectives. Some contemporary critics point to the limitations of his analyses, particularly regarding the exclusion of certain social groups and the lack of explicit consideration of the economic disparities resulting from the system he advocates. These criticisms resonate in current discussions on social justice and equity, highlighting the need for more inclusive approaches sensitive to diverse social realities.

Locke's influence on the liberal tradition and subsequent economic theories is undeniable. His defense of individual liberty, private property, and limited government contributed to shaping the principles that underpin many modern democracies. However, the direct applicability of his ideas in complex and interconnected economic contexts raises questions that continue to be explored and debated by contemporary scholars and thinkers. Ultimately, *Economic Writings* by John Locke remains a beacon in the history of economic and political thought. His ability to articulate a comprehensive vision that spans from the philosophical foundations of property to the practical implications of economic policies demonstrates a brilliant mind that transcends his time. The work continues to be a rich source of insights for those seeking to understand not only economic theory but also the complexities of interactions between individuals, government, and the market in contemporary societies.

Final Notes:

Throughout this book, we have explored the key ideas of John Locke in a simplified manner, aiming to understand how his works have impacted political philosophy and economic issues. Locke, one of the most influential thinkers of the Enlightenment, offered a new way of thinking about human nature, property, and government. His reflections on individual freedom, the right to property, and the social contract continue to be fundamental to understanding modern societies.

Locke believed that property is a natural right, derived from human labor and effort, and that legitimate government exists solely to protect these rights. His ideas on freedom and the consent of the governed provided the foundation for many principles of contemporary democracies. The notion that all individuals have equal and inalienable rights remains a central pillar in Western political thought.

By simplifying Locke's complex ideas, I hope the reader has gained a more accessible understanding of his philosophical contributions. Even though written centuries ago, his concepts still influence our political and social practices. As we reflect on his work, we are reminded of the importance of a government that respects individual freedom and fundamental rights, principles that remain vital in our current society.

Bibliographic references:

ALTMAN, Sam. OpenAI. Available at: https://openai.com/brand/. Accessed on: Jan 18, 2025.

ChatGPT. 2022. Available at: https://chatgpt.com/?model=auto. Accessed on: Jan 18, 2025.

PERKINS, Melanie. CANVA, 2025. Available at: https://www.canva.com/pt_br/. Accessed on: Jan 18, 2025.

Research GATE (2018). (PDF) John Locke's Educational Model: Moral, Utilitarian, and Empirical. Available at: https://www.google.com/url?sa=t&source=web&rct=j&opi=89978449&url=https://www publication/376543968_O_MODELO_EDUCACIONAL_DE_JOHN_LC pwqIJb. Accessed on: Jan 18, 2025.

VYRO LLC. IMAGINE AI, 2022. Available at: https://imagine.art/. Accessed on: Jan 18, 2025.

Be aware that these texts were partially generated by artificial intelligence and implemented in most of the work presented in this compendium. The citation of the logo and the respective name of the company OpenAI ("OpenAI, ChatGPT") is duly presented on the cover or early pages of the book, along with the logo and the respective name of the publisher and distributor.

Don't miss out!

Visit the website below and you can sign up to receive emails whenever Rodrigo v. santos publishes a new book. There's no charge and no obligation.

https://books2read.com/r/B-A-ULDBB-TMHAG

BOOKS2READ

Connecting independent readers to independent writers.

Also by Rodrigo v. santos

Compêndios da filosofia
Friedrich Nietzsche: Como a filosofia molda a ambição humana
Platão: como a filosofia molda a compreensão humana
George Hegel: Como a filosofia molda a consciência humana
John Locke: Como a filosofia molda a mente humana.

Philosophical compendiums
Friedrich Nietzsche: How Philosophy Shapes Human Ambition
Plato: How philosophy shapes human understanding.
Georg Hegel: How Philosophy Shapes Human Consciousness
John Locke: How Philosophy Shapes The Human Mind.